PUBLIC PRAYERS

PUBLIC PRAYERS

ARTHUR CUSHMAN McGIFFERT, Jr.

Exploration Press, Chicago

Printed in the United States of America

Exploration Press
Chicago Theological Seminary
5757 University Avenue
Chicago, Illinois 60637

ISBN: Paper: 0-913552-24-0

Library of Congress Catalog Number: 83-83269

Contents

FOREWORD

The concreteness of language which characterizes many of these prayers is a literary style I owe primarily to the example and teaching of Dr. Henry Sloan Coffin when he was minister of Madison Avenue Presbyterian Church in New York City and lecturer on Worship at Union Theological Seminary. I was a member of that church during my years in high school, and as a student at Union I took his course in Worship. In that course he used to say such things as "The bane of much public prayer is its generalities. Don't pray for people who are sick, pray for people who lie on beds of pain." "Instead of praying for lonely people, pray for those who long to have somebody speak to them or call on them." "Specific words are needed to grip the minds or kindle the imaginations of the congregation. It takes particular words to enlist feelings or conscience." Many of the statements Dr. Coffin made in class he subsequently included in his *The Public Worship of God, A Source Book for Leaders of Services,* Westminster Press, 1946.

With few exceptions the public prayers in this book have been delivered at Sunday morning services, at academic gatherings, and on other occasions at which people gather to express their deepest longings and satisfactions. Several of them have a long history, at least one of them having been composed in 1933. Some have undergone literary surgery, transplants and toning up.

In recent years I have come increasingly to recognize three other literary mentors, Ralph Waldo Emerson, for one. My mother Gertrude Huntington McGiffert also had an extraordinary sensitivity to words and thoroughly enjoyed (and worked at) putting them together in her verse and in her letters. Undoubtedly both my vocabulary and way of writing are also due in part to my father's crisp and clear style. In addition I owe to him the persisting foundation of my theology. All this past is prologue to the present. To the four prominent figures of my present, Elisabeth, David, Michael and Ellen, I dedicate these pages, with affection, appreciation and gratitude.

When my neighbor in Pilgrim Place, Eulalia Westberg (Mrs. D. D.) Williams learned that at long last I was proposing to prepare for publication a collection of my prayers, she begged me to let her type the manuscript. I gratefully and happily acquiesced, for it was Eulalia, then one of the secretaries at C.T.S. who shared in the typing of the manuscript of my first book, *Jonathan Edwards*.

ARTHUR CUSHMAN MCGIFFERT, JR.
Pilgrim Place, 1983

PASTORAL PRAYERS

PRAYING TOGETHER

Heavenly Father, these moments of praying together, how deep will they go? Shall we be able to get beneath the distracting surface of our life?

By the recollection of remembered friendships,
by some fugitive vision of splendor or delight,
by a word that has darted into our souls from hymn or scripture,
by a sense of wonder freshly evoked,
by an agony deep in the heart,
by some recall of our memories,
by an expectancy we have brought here,
by some tumultuous happiness,
by a hard-won decision,
by some frantic anxiety,
by an austere obligation that confronts us,
by the shocking realization of the emptiness of our lives,
by our terror before the crises of the day,
by the imagination of the needs of those present praying with us,
by our recognition that we stand in the need of prayer,

it may be—may it be—that, in solitude and in fellowship, we are making our way into the holy Presence,

abased and adoring,
judged and absolved,
broken and made whole,
cut loose and on course,
alone and companioned,
blinded and seeing thy face in the face of Jesus Christ.

A GOODLY COMPANY

Lift up our hearts, O God! Into thy presence we come worn, puzzled, bruised by the experiences of the weeks and the months. We have tried laughing at life, as though thou wast an unaccountable old jester, dealing us jolly punches in the side. But the laugh has turned to bitterness in our mouth. We have tried to pass life through the fire of our thinking and have seen that evil is partial only, that it is good in the making, that on the whole life is beautiful. And when we have been hurt, we have tried to reconcile ourselves to private loss and pain by thinking of the beneficence which on the whole obtains. Yet have we made sorry going of our philosophy.

We have tried to defy life, battling against its evils with the power of hate, returning malice for malice, only to discover that madness lies that way, for we become the very image of the thing we hate, and lose our humanness.

And sometimes desperately and faltering we have tried the way of righteousness, returning good for evil, bearing, serving, helping, trusting that all things work together for good. We have sought to relieve misery, to build up the constructive forces, to carry the full responsibilities of our position; to live by our hopes and not by our fears.

And we have been stirred by a strange and wild elation. We have found ourselves among a goodly company. We bless thee for them; those who, tender and true, are as the shadow of a great rock in a weary land; for those who in days of disaster still show themselves men and women of undaunted spirit, given to no impractical regrets, taking their place without bitterness in the great fraternity of troubled souls; for those who decline to add to the world's miseries a private quota of self-pity and suspicion; those for whom the commonplace appears rainbow-hued; for those who by their friendliness make more desirable, more accessible, the friend who sticketh closer than a brother, even Jesus Christ.

NAMELESS YET NAMED

O thou Nameless Being, whom yet we call by the most precious names men have invented, calling thee Father, Mother, Friend, and Lover, Judge Eternal robed in splendor, again in stammering feebleness would we try to tell thee what thou dost mean to us.

Thou meetest us on every hand,—in the beauties and bounties of nature, in the love which binds us to the living and the dead, in glimpses of truth, in the calls of duty, in our experiences of gladness and of grief, through the faith of thy servants of old and the devotion of thy servants at our side, in the quiet thoughts of our hearts and in the aspirations of this worshipping company. Draw aside the veils and set our spirits face to face with thee.

Thine eyes are in every place, for thy thoughts and love go out to all people. Send our minds and hearts abroad until we feel our kinship with the world-wide brotherhood of thy children and crave for all of them, as for ourselves, health of bodies, education that frees from superstition and ignorance, liberty to think and live as sons and daughters of God, a chance to work, a chance to rest, a conscience made sensitive by the insights of Jesus Christ, and a soul that trusts and serves thee in his spirit.

We pray for those whom thou hast given us to love and be loved by,—for small children, for men and women chilled in spirit by the atmosphere we create, for countless lives, unknown to us, but so linked with us in the web of existence that our fidelity to duty means life to them and our carelessness, loss. For their unknown sakes, sanctify us.

We pray for sad folks, sick folks, lonely folks, for those who feel their lives are wasted or their work futile or their spirits starved, that the fullness of Christ may be opened to them.

We pray for our country, that wisdom and public spirit may be plenteously bestowed upon the President and every citizen who bears a heavy burden of public responsibility; that our national character may be dominated by a spirit of service, that our land throughout its length and breadth and right here where we are, may be made glad by good will towards men. Give peace in our time, O Lord.

In the name of him who spoke of thee each time as if he had just left thy presence!

CHURCHES AND MINISTERS

ENERGY

Lord, for the churches of Jesus Christ, we bless thee, and for the spiritual energies issuing from them: energy of compassion, energy of public-mindedness, energy of self-respect, energy of self-discipline and self-sacrifice, energy of foresight, energy for foregiveness, energy of gratitude, energy of worship and service.

We confess the faults of our churches; their pretentions, their contentions, their contentedness, their conventionalities, their hesitance to adventure. We pray, nevertheless, that thou wilt be able to continue to use them for thy healing, judging, stimulating, enlightening, fellowshipping work among the children of men. Through them may the spirit of Christ find fresh entry to each of us and among us.

A HOUSE OF GOD

God of our fathers and our God, who dost commit to each generation the task of keeping thy church strong for Christian service, we give thee thanks for this fellowship and our part in its enduring and sustaining life.

We bless thee for this building, the work of many hands across the years, into which so much imagination and daring and generous care have been put.

We bless thee for those who here in infancy and youth have been welcomed as members of the household of faith.

We bless thee for lives here united in mutual affection, forbearance and re-enforcement.

We bless thee for all those who have gathered here for the last tender service of faith and love.

We bless thee for the Christian ministries that here day after day are planned, begun and carried through,—feeding the hungry, welcoming the stranger, clothing the naked, visiting the sick, invading the community with compassion and good will.

We bless thee for the friendships with which the church enriches our lives, for the loyalties it calls forth, for the self-discipline it lays upon our tempers, the aspirations it arouses, the grounding it gives our feet on a rock that cannot be shaken; for the ties that bind it to the far-off quarters of the globe; for the host of patient endeavors going out from it to build the mind of Christ into home and neighborhood and nation; and above all, for that constant source of spiritual contagion and courage which comes from him who sanctified himself for others' sake.

WE PRAISE THE LORD

HOLY, HOLY, HOLY

Thou hast set eternity in our hearts, O God. We are not as those who have no shrine. Deeply lodged in our minds is thy holy image—mysterious, fascinating, awe-full—commanding our devotion, compelling us to trust in truth, in loveliness, in duty. Thou art the Holy One, standing apart, uplifted. Thou art God. It is thou that speakest; we listen. It is for thee to use us, not for us to use thee. Thou art God; we are servants. Grant that our restless hearts may find their rest in thee.

EYESIGHT

Lord, we have eyes to see with, most of us. We have glasses or spectacles that enable many of us to see better.

Yet our eyesight has become blurred during the week, our seeing is dimmed or out of focus.

Restore our sight that we may see ourselves, that we may see others through the eyes of Jesus Christ.

SPRING TIME

Great art thou, O Lord, our God!

How small this patch of the earth where we live! How close the horizon!

Yet all about us such power,—power of seeds opening, power of branches putting out leaves inch by inch, power of stalks and stems soon to burst into flowers, power of roots making new tunnels in the soil; energy of loyalty in our homes, energy of responsibilities taken on, the animation of thinking, the propulsion of sympathies, the dynamic of loving and being loved, the momentum of memory.

All these forces are part of thy Almightiness. Thine are the kingdom and the power and the glory!

THE VISIBLE AND THE INVISIBLE

Eternal God, renew in us the assurance of that invisible world which environs us with its spiritual persuasions. The blessings which surround our favored lives sometimes by their abundance shut out this wider view. Our homes, our plans, our work, our play, the absorbing interest of our cares and joys, how they confine our thoughts! Open our eyes that we may see the sustaining environment of thy love and law; and through the things which are temporal may we discern the things which are eternal.

Keep open the far horizons of the Eternal. May the glare of lamps about us not shut out the light of the stars. And when in brief glimpses the meaning of life is disclosed, or our homes are sanctified by joy or sorrow, or the pressure of work is relaxed, or the world of opportunity calls for generous service, may these disclosures of a larger life reveal to us thy beneficent guidance; and our daily prayer be that we may not be disobedient to that heavenly vision, which we have come to know in and through the mind of Christ.

FAIREST LORD JESUS

Lord, thou hast made life beautiful for us, so that even those who seem most miserable, love life because they cannot bear to lose sight of such a beautiful and lovely world.

Thou hast given us eyes to see the shining beauty of day-light, the dark beauty of night, "the mystery of color, the might of design"; inward eyes to see the beauty of love which brightens our common life.

All things lovely are a part of thy revealing.

Thy most successful expression is he who prized lilies of the field and birds of the air, whose beauty is the beauty of holiness, whose name is Wonderful, whose wondrous cross consecrates all love that suffers long and is kind, whose living and dying disclose the breadth and length, the height and depth of loving,—fairest Lord Jesus.

WE GIVE THANKS

EVERYDAY SAINTS

I

We bless thee for one and another, known to us, whose spirits have an inner sparkle, for those who in disillusioning days keep a good heart, whose faith rises over prostrating circumstances, who are not at the mercy of the things that befall them for they have an inner chamber of fortitude reinforced by thee.

We bless thee for those who remind us that it is still good to be honest and not a scamp; still good to seek knowledge and not be ignorant; still good to face life with courage and not run away from difficulties; indisputably good to be considerate and public-minded; for those who give little thought to thy being useful to them, so absorbed are they in trying to be useful to thee.

For the light of the knowledge of thy glory in the face of Jesus Christ, we bless thee. Make us sons and daughters of thy light and thy joy.

II

Through silent tears, Lord, we thank thee for those who have lived through the singing season, and e'er the days of sorrow and handicap have gone on ahead, never knowing the dim December of life but only the blithe springtime and the harvest season; for those who tread the road of life with head uplifted and a smiling face, even through the dark valley; for those so splendidly unhindered by the things that hold us back; for all integrity of mind and generosity of temper and all acceptance of responsibility; for those who build their lives into a family or an institution and so go on helping and serving through the generations that follow.

III

Grateful are we, Lord, for the wit and whimsy of those who are aware of the comic side of life, minds that cavort, minds allowed to go on a lark; for those who deal with death as an intrinsic part of life, who know that though *life* is Time's fool, *love* is not Time's fool, for the gift of love is immortality; for those whose finished lives have the shape of completeness about them.

IV

Praise be to thee, Lord, for the rich delight of well-furnished minds, for many-storied, towering minds, minds searching and inventive, minds seminal and frontier-crossing, minds which inhabit at one and the same time the past, the present and the future; for intellectual enthusiasms; for those who have gladly embraced the disciplines of learning and define the scholar for us.

V

Lord, we bless thee for those for whom the wrinkled face of the earth is a magnet, drawing to it foot and mind alike; in whose ears sounds the far call of mountains, luminous and clear, mountains that stretch extended, tall, mountains that curl up in a coil.

We bless thee for eyes which discern colors and patterns withheld from duller sight; for the artist's gift of seeing, and for those through whose eyes we have seen heaven on earth.

UNPROFITABLE SERVANTS

I

We venture into thy holy presence, not worthy to present ourselves before thee. For thou art Truth—but every day of our lives is cracked by insincerity and deceit. Thou art the everlasting Goodness—but our conscience convicts us of being ill-tempered, intolerant, and careless. Thou art Love, long-suffering and kind, love that demands justice, love that forgives—and we hug our self-conceit, we wall off those who might claim our sympathy, we fear to take a stand for fair play. We are thy unprofitable servants.

And yet, Lord, still would we be thy servants, for without thee our lives are nothing. We perish without truth, without goodness, without love,—without thee.

Restore our souls. Intensify the grip upon us of life's sanctities. Open the doors of our spirits that the imprisoned splendors may escape.

II

We, who are creatures of a few decades, whose years are like shadows lying on sunny hills, turn to thee, the Rock of Ages.

We think of all we call "nature": this earth with its skin of prairies and sea, the life therein, trees gripping the soil with their roots, tiny creatures, stars and nebulae—smallness and vastness beyond imagination. All these operating according to their laws, their growth, their regularities, their rhythm. So much there is to wonder at—yet how often the windows of our imagination have been shuttered.

Thee we love, O God. Thy name is Truth, and we have known occasions when truth has made us free,—free from self-reproach, free from having to calculate our next statement, free to enjoy the confidence of others. Thy truth we love. Yet must we confess that we have cut corners. We suppress. We hug our self-conceit that whispers to us, "Never mind the truth; comfort and popularity are what you want."

We stand ready to serve thee and please thee in the place where we are, with such gifts as we have: to do each day's duty, to serve thee with our minds, to be friendly, to carry out the trusts we have assumed, to be generous, to stand for human freedom against tyranny, to fulfill the obligations of our citizenship, developing the talents within us. Yet we do confess that we have often run away from responsibility, we have put ourselves first, we have indulged our own whims, we have let our talents go, we have even questioned the value of living. We have felt that our only policy is to struggle with might and main for ourselves by snatching what we can. What unprofitable servants we are!

NO IMAGINATION

Lord, how conscious we are of our obtuseness! How perilous has been our lack of imagination!

Thou should'st be to us a daily companion, like one who gives a lift along a weary road, like a glorious picture that smooths away our cares, like the encouraging smile of a friend that stimulates and kindles us. And instead we take thee for granted and neglect thee as though thou didst not exist.

And how carelessly we sometimes treat our friends, as though they would be with us forever, like so much furniture, like the fence posts on our way to work.

The thought of home brings us tightening of the heart, no thrills.

We fail to hold either home, or friends or thee intensely in our minds.

Grant that right now, this minute, with loving imagination, with delight, with devotion and with marvelling, we may think of home. . . . . of friends. . . . . . . and of thee. . . . .

THE DIVINE ENEMY

Judge of the sons of men—who dost set before us a way that is hard, a way that is difficult to manage, requiring us to subordinate our wayward desires to the rule of thy right and they goodness,—at times thou art hateful in our sight. We want to have our own way, not thy way. Thou thwartest us. Thou dost beset us before and behind with many an obstacle to our inclinations. We do not want the real; we want to escape into the unreal where we may live according to our fancy, where we may make our own terms with life and not have life demanding that we surrender to its terms.

Canst thou not leave us alone, O God? How is it that even though we make our bed in hell, thou art there, relentless Judge, ever at the back of thy runaways? Canst thou not transform thyself into a good fairy, a lucky stone, become the Open Sesame for our desires? Then should we welcome thee as the darling of our heart, as now we denounce thee as our great antagonist.

How shall we deal with thee? Can we love thee, thou divine Enemy? Yes,—is that the secret, that when we love our enemies, even thee, O God, thou becomest for us a friend? As we accept thy way, yielding ourselves to thee as Fact, we escape from fairyland and find that in thy law is liberty; in thy truth is light; in thy beauty are poise and power.

IDOLS

We know, Lord, that thou art God. And we do not know it.

We know that thou has made us and not we ourselves. And we do not know it.

We know that, except the Lord build the house, they labor in vain that build it. And we do not know it.

We know that thou art the God not only of those whose skin is the same color as ours. And we don't know even this.

O Lord, the idols we have put in thy place,—such engrossing idols, such pleasant idols, such comfortable idols! How they cast their spell upon us: spell of self-sufficiency, spell of prejudice, spell of narrow-mindedness, spell of irresponsibility, spell of special privilege. All these idols! Them we know all too well!

Lord, stab our spirits wide awake, in recognition and shame.

May each one of us now, separately and yet aware of all the other idolaters in this room, acknowledge a particular idol we have sneaked into this service of worship, and call it by its rightful name.

Lord, open our ear to hear the voice of thy commanding Love, thy commanding Justice, thy commanding Truth, saying unto us, unto each "me" here, "Thou shalt have no other Gods before me."

Lord, may we come to our Christian senses!

FOR THOSE PRAYING WITH US

Father, we pray for those who are praying:
for those whose prayer is a kind of poetry in their nature, a music in the soul, a cleaving of the sky on joyful wing, a meeting with an invisible Companion, an overflowing of the heart's gratitude and praise.
We pray for those whose prayer is like an army with banners.
We pray for those whose prayer is a small thought holding immeasurable vastness in its hands, a gathering up of the long memory which is the church, an opening of the desert of the soul to the fountains of thy living water.
We pray for those whose praying is the joy of elevated thought, for those in the handicraft of whose work is their prayer.
We pray for those whose prayer, at the extremity of their strength, is a probing deep down within themselves, scraping the very bone of existence; for those whose prayer is a faint whisper as they enter the valley of the shadow of death.
We pray for those too tired, too discouraged, too vanquished by doubts, too uncertain of life's meaning, to pray.
We pray for those cast down, who yet thirst for thee, the Living God; for those whose prayer is no language but a cry; for those conscious of the stain with which their past has marked their lives whose prayer is in the self-accusative case; for those whose prayer is a listening to the still, sad voice of humanity, a secret battlefield of the spirit, an acquiescence to thy Will, a recommitment of themselves to the Shepherd of their souls.

AN INTERNATIONAL PRAYER

O thou, from whom the whole family in heaven and on earth is named, we who are children of earth turn to thee in the agony of our differences of race and nation. Many are the colors of our skins; of one color, our blood. Remind us that it is thou who hast made of this one blood all nations to dwell upon the face of the earth. Thou are our common Father. Thou knowest what we so often fail to remember and shamefully deny,—that we are all brethern.

We are not as people without a country. We love our own land. Yet we confess that when some of our fellow-citizens pipe unto us, we cannot dance to the uncritical measures of their patriotic songs. Save us from forgetting that our citizenship is also in heaven. How can be maintain our dual citizenship, O Lord? Verily we are pilgrims and sojourners as our fathers were. Help us to play the man and serve thee in the places where we now are.

O God of peace, we pray for peace. Unite us with all others who call upon the Lord of peace, whether in friendly or in hostile tongues. Let justice roll down as waters upon this torn earth, and righteousness as a mighty stream. Establish thou the work of our hands, the work of peace, upon us. Thou canst make the wrath of man to praise thee.

Give power to us who faint. To us, peace-lovers and peacemakers, increase our strength. Out of the depth of our distress, we cry to thee. We use, to our comfort, the ancient words of Scripture. Restore to us a sense of comradeship with those, our human enemies but not our enemies in Christ, who also pray for peace. Suffer not our contradictory wills for victory to have their way, except thy will for peace be done thereby, for thine alone are the kingdom and the power and the glory.

FOR PEOPLE OF MIDDLE AGE

Our prayer, Lord, is for those for whom the years of middle age have become increasingly difficult. The self-confidence of youth has slackened and the serenity of old age has not arrived. The demands of life have become monotonous and wearisome to them.

Save them from the temptations of these middle years,—sense of futility, loss of joy. Lead them from the flatness of depression and self-contempt to the high places of opportunity which thou hast reserved for those who stand between youth and age.

Rescue them from the hypocrisies of social life and from the refuge of cynicism. Enable them to hear afresh the call for generous and self-effacing service. Direct them in their search for the spiritually efficient life until the True, the Good, the Beautiful, witnesses of thy presence, sustain them,—and the middle years become not the Dark Age but an Age bright with satisfactions and contentment, unattained by youth and to be treasured for old age.

FOR PEOPLE WHO ARE GROWING OLD

Lord, we pray for those who each day find it more difficult to pick up the piece of their lives and put them in place;

for those who walk by the memories of their yesterdays;

for those who, encompassed about with their dear dead, make the distant heaven a home for their hearts;

for those who have been able to accept the grim inevitabilities of their years,

who, despite their age, are still young people inhabiting old bodies;

who exploit the weakness of their age by the over-demands they make on others;

who still find some reason for getting up in the morning;

for the darkened windows of old eyes;

for those whose thoughts have all been thought, so they no longer enjoy solitude;

who gaze upon instruments and tools they once so lovingly used, whose hands now fail them;

those for whom the greetings of young friends have become too rough; who find it very hard sometimes to realize how intensely they are loved and of what value their presence is to those who love them;

for those whose dwelling place has shrunk to four gray walls and one green window space;

who once could laugh at themselves but for whom the laugh has become more wry, more grim, until it has ceased to be a laugh at all, but a curse;

who dread becoming a burden to others;

who accept enforced leisure without a sense of guilt, if not with gusto;

for those who are engaged in heart-aching readjustments because of a loved one's death;

for those whose salt has not lost its savor and who still take themselves with a grain of it;

who in their later years are treated more and more like a child, yet still do their best not to act in childish ways;

those whose arteries are hardening but there is no hardening of the heart;

who are content with made work when they can no longer carry on the kind of work that once defined their lives;

who do not dissipate their diminishing strength on trivialities;

for those for whom aging means, not going to pieces, but going in pieces;

those who look at us with bleak misery in their eyes;

for those who smile to themselves, remembering how their lot had been cast in pleasant places, whose fate it had been to leave their careers amidst the good words and the loving kindness of devoted friends, and who mutter to themselves, Lord, now lettest thou thy servant depart in peace, Lord, now lettest thou thy servant depart in peace.

FOR THOSE WHO MOURN

Lord, we pray for those whose turn it is again to undergo the slow, healing work of mourning: the shock, the numbness, the helplessness, the isolation, the terror and despair, the altered sense of time, the untying of the knots of habits, the emptiness, the collapse. Blessed be those who in their work of mourning go on to grieve. Theirs the sorrow and the sadness, the tears and angers, the lamentations and bitter second thoughts of loss, an anguished heart, a soul hard hit, cast down, bent almost to the breaking point, yet straightening slowly up. Blessed are those whose final work of mourning is the acceptance of loss, the re-taking up of life's activities, the recovery of balance between solitude and society, the re-collection of their powers, the re-investment of their affection and energy, the training of themselves in new habits to replace those no longer appropriate or needed. Theirs no longer the difficult language of unaccustomed things. Instead of the old song there is a new song in their hearts, as they have come to know at last that blessed are they that mourn for they shall be comforted.

MINISTRY

Grant, O Lord, that we who belong to the profession of the ministry may enjoy its fellowship, knowing ourselves to be a part of a common work, with shared interests. We thank thee for opportunities for growth this ministry offers us, so that we dare put our best selves into it, refraining from what is sham and shallow. Give us that sense of the urgency of crucial issues, so that we gladly engage in the fight for Christian justice and truth, in heart and mind, and among people. Keep us receptive to new accents of thy voice within us. Deliver us from the temptations of the ministry,—the temptation to be corrupted by our friends, the lure of publicity, the loss of touch with people, laziness, self-righteousness and the claim for special privilege. Remind us of why we are ministers. Why? Because we have been summoned into this profession not to be served, but to serve.

AT THE INSTALLATION OF A MINISTER

Lord, bless this new adventure here and now begun. Let there grow up between this minister and this people a mutual respect. Enable them soon to discover that they can trust each other. Enable him to speak the truth in love and live out the truth in patience. Let them bear each other on their hearts in prayer, as partners in a common enterprise. As together they shall seek thy face, give them fresh visions to which they cannot but commit themselves. Yea, as together they shall wait upon thee, may they renew their strength, mount up with wings as eagles, run and not weary, walk and not faint. Bless this minister and this congregation. Keep them. Make thy face to shine upon them. Be gracious unto them. Lift up the light of thy countenance upon them. Give them peace.

FOR CHURCHES

We pray for churches throughout the world,—for their truth, their unity and their stability; and for our own church, that what is unsound in it may be corrected and what is lacking may be supplied. Give us the patience to understand those Christians from whom we differ, since we bear a common name and serve a common master. Help us to respect them when we disagree with the truths for which they stand and to differ from them, when we must, in Christian love.

IN THE EVENING

As the hours of daylight come to an end, our Father,, we remember those who must stay awake that we may sleep; those who keep vigil against fire and crime and whatsoever evil or peril walks in the darkness. To thine unslumbering care we commend those who through the night hours carry on our restless commerce by land and our dangerous trafficking by sea. We thank thee for all these unknown men and women, and crave thy forgiveness if our thoughtlessness or love of comfort add to their toll and risk of life. Their tasks being made safe, may they find thee in the watches of the night.

IN BEHALF OF SOCIAL ACTION

Father, because we have discovered that one way to love thee is to seek to promote justice in the public order, we bless thee for the gathering momentum of our common social actions.

As the days ahead unfold, keep wide our horizons, deepen our understandings, strengthen our devotion, hearten our courage in the face of crises, sustain our perseverance over the long pull,—remembering that those who are for us and those who are against us are equally thy children; thine, not ours, the power, the kingdom and the glory.

WE PRAY FOR OURSELVES

AS WE ARE

O thou, God of our salvation, save us from ourselves,—from the vulgarity of pretense, from the impertinence of pride, whether it be pride of family, pride of social standing, pride of achievement,—save us from the prides that harden our sympathies and warp our judgments.

Save us from our past. The harm we have done to others rises up in our memories and accuses us,—the heat of angry passions, the secret lusts of eye and heart. Even the voice of prayer cannot bring back the glow of young ideals we have chilled by our cynical words, nor restore the brightness of those whose hearts have been darkened because they have encountered us on their way.

Grant that a humbler and purer life may grow out of our contrition, that henceforth we may bring comfort and encouragement where we have scorned and crushed. Change us from being sources of evil into sources of good. Grant us the mercy of a valiant heart that we may tread the road of life with head uplifted and a smiling face, doing our work to the last with faith and hope and love. Deliver us from our reluctance to recognize the standards of thy Kingdom, and deliver us from our unwillingness to try to live by them in home and shop and study. Lead us to expect great things of thee and to achieve at least something for thee.

THE THORNY NETTLE

Lord, with the Psalmist we, too, ask: "What is man that thou are mindful of him?"

We know that we are creatures of a day; yet thou hast set eternity in our hearts. Our spirits so easily bruise; yet thou hast made available to us the good comfort of love. We are puzzled and daunted by the disasters that befall us; yet thou dost companion us as we march breast-forward. If we grasp life's thorny nettle, it becomes for us thy holy rose. When the clock of our life strikes the hour of trouble and we can say, "to meet this hour was I born into the world", then, slowly, patience and power and endurance re-occupy our minds. This is thy Providence,—that as our days so shall our strength be. Thus thou dost no longer remain for us an enemy, whom we hate, but a friend and saviour. The things which are seen are temporal and pass away. The unseen things are spiritual and eternal.

What are we? Sons and daughters of whom thou art mindful.

FOR PEACE

O God, we whose hopes are so often broken, turn to thee for refreshment and restoration. The Creator, the everlasting God will not faint. *Thou* wilt not grow weary.

We who so easily become cynical about peace, now seek in holy imagination the company of the Great Hearts of the world, thy patient saints, thy buoyant fellow-workers, the blessed peace-makers of the ages,—hearts of courage, all of them.

Our first duty is to hope. Our final need is courage.

Be still to us the God of good Hope; be still for us the Captain of Victory.

IN THE DOLDRUMS

Lord, we are not in need of greater marvels round us, nor of a more wonderful world, nor of larger opportunities of service, nor of further occasions of joy. But at this time, when awareness of them has slackened, at this time when sorrow or loss or anxiety or uncertainty becloud our souls, grant us the grace of recalling times when there were few clouds. May the remembering of those experiences of marvel, of wonder, of service, of joy keep hope alive for us during this darkened time.

SPECIAL OCCASIONS

FOR A BAPTISM

Eternal Spirit, before whose face the generations rise and pass away and without whom we can neither live nor move nor have our being, Lord of heaven and earth, God and Father of every human heart! Keep this little child of ours sound of body, sunny in disposition, clear and active in mind. Set eternity in his heart.

As he grows up, give breadth to his interests, length to his aims, depth to his convictions and height to his ideals. Endow him with a stout head and a steady hand. May the door of his heart be always on the latch. Keep him from measuring himself by mean standards and so imagining that he is wiser or better than his fellows. Inspire him to do justly, love mercy and walk reverently with thee, so that generations yet unborn will cherish the choicer things of life because of his joy in living.

Bless him, dear Lord, make the face of thy purpose, the magnetism of thy truth, the reinforcement of thy love shine upon him and give him courage and peace.

AT THE LORD'S TABLE

We venture into thy presence, Lord, not worthy to present ourselves before thee, for thou art Truth,—but every day of our life has been cracked with insincerity and deceit.

Thou are the everlasting Goodness,—and our conscience convicts us of meanness, intolerance and carelessness.

Thou art Love, long-suffering, kind, love which presses for justice, love which forgives,—and we have hugged our self-conceit, we have walled off those who might claim our compassion, we have been afraid to take a stand for the right.

Yet still, Lord, are we trying to be thy servants, for without thee our lives are nothing. We perish without love, without goodness, without truth, without thee.

Revive our drooping spirits, Enliven our consciences, Take away the dimness of our souls; intensify the grip upon us of life's sanctities. Open for us the ways by which they imprisoned splendor may break through.

Refresh us as we shall eat and drink at the Lord's table, as his guests.

EASTER

Eternal father of our souls, who art from everlasting to everlasting, in praise re-echoed by exultant hearts of multitudes on this Day of Days, we, too, unite in joyful celebrating.

We acknowledge in awe our transciency. Dust of the earth our bodies are and unto dust shall they return. Yet what is this dust we cannot fully understand. We have seen it stirred by every little seed and root under the softening rain until life in silence again weaves robes of grain for the fields, colors the garden beds, trees burst into green loveliness. Intimations of our human immortality the advancing spring-time gives us.

With reverent expectancy we yield ourselves to the majestic thought of life eternal. We listen to the hopeful words of Jesus. We welcome the declaration of his disciples. Death, they said, had no dominion over him; it is not possible that death could control him.

Something within us, too, "leaps life's narrow bars
to claim its birthright with the hosts of heaven;
a gladness fed with secret tears,
a vexing, forward-reaching sense
of some more noble permance,
a light across the sea
which haunts our soul and will not let it be."

We repeat the assurance that what is excellent, as God lives, is permanent. May these forecasts become a continuous and sustaining hope, the venture of faith, the consolation of sorrow, the contact of our lives with eternity. So may we anticipate the future that awaits us and practice our immortality by the conquest of the spirit over the flesh, by the restraint of passion, by companionship with lives that were not made to die.

We bless thee for that company, near and dear to us, who have faithfully lived and peacefully died; for all fair memories and fond hopes, we bless thee. Hearts may be remote yet not asunder; and as we pray it is as though many unseen bowed and prayed with us.

"They come transfigured back,
Secure from change in their high-hearted ways,
Beautiful evermore and with bright rays of hope
On their white shields of expectation."

PRE-CHRISTMAS

Giver of every good and perfect gift, brighten us with the thought of happy memories. We are glad that out of our abundance we can make others happy. We are glad that children's faces can light up, and that we can bring happy tears into their eyes. We thank thee for home and childhood and for all the dear human fellowships and friends. We thank thee for those whose joys are not at the mercy of what may happen to them,—neither other people's hostility, nor the adversity of circumstance. We thank thee for every star of hope. Above all we thank thee for him whose birth we shall celebrate, who belongs to no one nation, to no one race, to no one group. His line is gone out throughout the earth and his circuit unto the ends of it. Magi and shepherds together praise him, learned and ignorant praise him, toilers of brain and toilers of hand praise him. Hasten the time when the love that he showed to thee and the love that he showed to people, yea, love even unto death, may bring about peace on earth. And to that end may Christ be born in us this coming Christmas Day.

CHRISTMAS

Lord, so often we have prayed a Christmas prayer.
In times of war, in times of peace,
in times of happiness, in times of anxiety,
in times of perplexity, in times of confidence,
in times when the future opened inviting ways,
in times when the shadows lengthened and the evening of life has come,
in times of laughter and in times of tears,
in times of loneliness, in times of families gathered together, at home, away from home, homeless—no matter where, no matter what,
we have prayed a Christmas prayer,—
a prayer of thanks for the gift of God who guides and enriches and adds power to our living and prompts our giving,—
a Christmas prayer that turns into a song,—
a song whose theme is a baby,
a song about a little town called Bethlehem,
a song that came upon a midnight clear, a glorious song of old,
a song of a star with beams so bright, more lovely than the noon-day light,
a song about a star of wonder,
a song about a rose, e'er blooming, that came a flower bright,
an echo of herald angels singing, Glory to God in the highest and on earth peace, good will to men,

the theme song of faith and hope and love.
But never mind the song. It is the singing that counts, joyful people, triumphant people, faithful people singing,—a Christmas prayer.
We, too!

CHILDREN'S SUNDAY

How glad we are, God, that we can think about mountains and oceans, about trees and flowers, and boats and the mysterious wind,—whenever we want to; about stories we have read, and pictures we like and people who love us. When we stop to think about it, we realize that we couldn't be half what we are if it weren't for fathers or mothers or a very special friend who believe in us and really expect us to do our best. Help us not to disappoint them too much.

We remember, even though we wish we didn't, how often we have given up and not finished something we began, and then made up all kinds of silly excuses. Yet thou hast given us strong bodies and we are able to think, just so that we may be able to do things that are hard to do.

Sometimes we are so careless. We pay no attention to how people are feeling. We forget they have feelings. We hurt our friends by saying words we really didn't mean. When we feel tired and let other people do things for us, we forget that perhaps they are just as tired as we are and are having a hard time not to let their cross feelings show on the outside.

We think of those who at school and out of school are trying to do the right thing and to play fair, when others around them are becoming popular by doing things that are unfair, or a bit tricky or plain wrong. Help us and help the others, when this kind of temptation comes, to keep in plain sight fair-play and kindness and self-respect.

We pray for boys and girls who have to work for long hours when they aren't really old enough to do so; for boys and girls who are sick and cannot go outdoors; for children who are deaf and can't hear the voices and the sounds we hear, who are blind and can't see the light and the colors we can see; for boys and girls who are handicapped and cannot run or jump; for girls and boys who have no father or mother; for those who are sad and puzzled and scared because their friend has gone away on a strange journey which is called death; for those who have no baby sister or brother to play with; for those who are away from home and feel homesick; for those who know nothing about that wonderful man whose name is Jesus.

What nerve he had! How gentle he was! How he could sympathize! How he could endure hard things! What a good story teller he was!

We are glad we know the prayer he taught people so many years ago. People have been saying it ever since, and now, think of it, we are going to say it too!

Our Father. . . . .

FOR THE CHURCH SCHOOL

For teachers and pupils, Lord, we pray. For the boys and girls who gather here, may this school be a place of happy companionships, maturing convictions, and widening activities. Here may they learn the rich heritage of the Christian centuries, the world's sore needs, the fellowship of the church. Here may their lives be caught up in the faith and hope and love of Jesus Christ. With each year's growth may they put away childish things, fearing only what is wrong, loving what is right, ready with clean hands and pure hearts to enter into a world that needs their help. Here may they learn to gather up their successes and their failures, and all their desires into simple prayer.

For those who, week by week, carry on the sacred ministry of teaching, renew the vision of service which first beckoned them to their work. Hear their prayer:

"Lord, who are we to show the way
To little children day by day,
So prone ourselves to go astray?
We teach them knowledge yet we know
How faint they flicker and how low
The candles of our knowledge glow.
We teach them love for all mankind
And all God's creatures yet we find
Our love comes lagging far behind.
Lord, if their guide we still must be,
O let the little children see
Their teacher leaning hard on thee."

GIFTS

Grant that the causes to which these gifts of ours will be devoted may prosper under thy guidance,—to the benefit of humankind, the advancement of thy kingdom and the glory of thy name.

Remember in thy love those who have brought these gifts, and those to whom they will be given. So follow these our offerings with they blessing that they may promote good will and peace, here at home and among people round the world, and thus advance the kingdom of the Lord Jesus Christ.

WEDDINGS

FOR A WEDDING

O Thou, who settest the solitary together in families which transcend the years and yet for whom each day is precious, for the new ties here established, loyalties focussed, springs of affection deepened, we bless thee. May love flow between these two dear people, unstinted, unstopped. Bind them together by the experiences they will share. As from time to time they come close to the heart of things that cannot be spoken, give them the gift of subtle communication. Advance them steadily in the discovery that what is most important is not what each has been alone, but what they now are and will be together.

May they become experts in quiet courtesies day by day. Save them from carelessly hurting each other's feelings. Reinforce the structure of their affections by happy companionships and outgoing activities. Teach them the law of partnership with others so that they will enlarge the circle of their concerns and keep in circulation the talents they go abundantly possess. Save them from the pitfalls of their privileges.

Encourage them, as they shall seek to serve thee in whatever place they are, to carry through the obligations they will assume, to be obedient to the unenforceable; to stand for human freedom against tyranny, for justice against favoritism or neglect. Enable them to play their part in the life of our time with imagination and steadfastness. So may the communities in which they shall live become more vital and more vivid, because of their citizenship.

May theirs be the joy of being trusted, theirs the inner reward of being looked to for strength to lean on, theirs the zest of creating order out of chaos, theirs the delight of dissipating dullness with vitality and sparkle.

Lord, help them that they may be a blessing and a comfort, each to the other, sharers of each other's joys, consolers of each other's sorrows, helpers of each other in all the chances and changes of the world.

May the home here and now begun be for them a harbor and a horizon, a sanctuary in time of storm, a place whence issue valiant service to their generation. In their new home may faith and hope and love be conjoined,—faith, the foundation of life, hope, the food for tomorrow, love, the tight cord of every day and beyond our days.

FUNERALS*

I

Lord of heaven and earth, God and Father of every human heart, we praise thee for this fair world and for the changing seasons. Thou dost bless both seed time and harvest and all the silent mysteries of growth. With each fresh spring morning give us joy in work and play, in home and friends, and with each day's ending give us grateful hearts.

We bless thee:

For those whose eyes are open to the loveliness of the world; for their happy recognition of romance in words, in colors, and in human affections;

for honest minds, honest with themselves and with others; candid to face the issues of life and unflinchingly to accept its realities;

for those who steer a delicate course between cynicism and sentimentality; who never try to appear something they are not;

for the wholesome astringencies of common sense;

for those who give short shrift to cant and conceit, impatient of pretense, who delight in puncturing the hypocrisies of a surface piety;

for all forthrightness and fortitude;

for those who go forward unflinchingly when the road is hard;

for grit and gumption that make life positve rather than passive;

for those who, as they grow older, do not grow stale in interests nor obsolete in opinions; whose spirits never bleach out into pale and neutral tints;

for gaiety of mind and wit;

for cheerfulness of heart that doeth good like medicine;

for all stern and stubborn pride in great traditions; for the sense of *noblesse oblige*;

for those who have a discerning sympathy for young people seeking to find their way in the world;

for those who decline to linger in profitless forebodings;

for those who industriously cultivate the arts of friendship, and having shown themselves friendly, have many friends;

for those whose fireside is a magnet for the lonely and the jaded, as well as for familiar companions;

*The length of the funeral prayers is explained by the fact that they were delivered at services in which there were no memorial addresses. They celebrated four intimate friends: a relative of the preceding generation, a college class-mate, the wife of a close ministerial colleague, a one-time academic colleague.

for those who hold high and firm the family roof-tree; whose deep-flowing loyalty to home becomes a shining benediction;
for lives enriched by children and children's children; yea, many rise up and call them blessed;
for those who put themselves under their own burdens cheerfully and without show, and under the burdens of others with quiet helpfulness;
for those who have not asked thee to do for them what they could and should do for themselves;
for all patience under the pressure of life's mysteries;
for those whose spirits have bowed in worship in this house and gotten here a new grip on this strange business of living and dying; who have shared in the fellowship of this church;
for those who in the midst of quickly passing time have found the eternity thou hast set in their hearts;
for the peace that comes to worn-out bodies as spirit explores the unimaginable shores.

We lift up to these our own memories, memories that scar,—our failures in affection, our faulty perspectives, the words we have failed to say, the gestures of affection we have omitted to make;—memories also that cleanse; memories that strengthen and comfort; memories that bind our hearts closer together.

"Life and death, thy creatures, praise thee, Mighty Giver.
Life nor death can part us, O thou Love Eternal,
Shepherd of the wandering star and souls that wayward flee,
Homeward draws the spirit to thy spirit yearning,—
Who were, and art, and evermore shalt be."

II

Eternal God, as we have gathered here for this last tender service of faith and hope and love, we turn to thee who art the Lord of heaven and earth, the God and Father of every human heart. Still, the heavens declare thy glory. Thy living power pulsates in every living thing. In thee all things are held together. How magnificent thou art!

In vivid memory, in yearning recollection, in loving pride, in sorrow of heart, yet in quiet confidence, we lift to thee the life of our friend and well-beloved.

We bless thee, Lord,
for integrity of mind and liveliness of spirit,
for good judgment and courage and trustworthiness,
for readiness to accept responsibility, to assume the obligations of citizenship,

We bless thee
for those whose cheerful heart doeth good like medicine,
for those aware of the comic side of life, who have an eye for its absurdities,
for those who omit no delicate attention of friendship,
for quiet courtesies and day-to-day companionability,
for those who give their hearts and wills into love's fearless keeping,— not in vain,
for far-reaching minds, well-furnished minds,
for lovers of books who cherish sequestered hours in their company,
for the artist-gift of seeing, eyes open to the loveliness of things, who tether spirit, clothing it in line and color,
for the gifted hand.
We bless thee
for those who like to slip into the world of music which never grows old for them, lovers of patterns of sounds, of melodic ideas that haunt the heart,
for those who, listening to music, hear their own hearts sing,
for those who touch the keys and a spell is cast,
We bless thee
for those in whose eyes our eyes have seen heaven,
for all shining hours when for us, too the world is a glory and a flame,
for all places glorified by love's old securities,
for the grip of tasks love shares and dignifies,
for family life, the rewards, the prides, the fun of belonging,— fathers and mothers, sons and daughters, uncles and aunts, grandsons and granddaughters, children and babies;
for all home cheer and helping that have notched the memory with happiness,
for those who have discovered that home is where the spirit dwells, the heart remembers, there are no farewells.

We lift to thee this experience of bereavement as a mould into which each of us pours our own private brief and shared glory.

"Blessed are they that mourn, for they shall be comforted.

"Life nor death can part us, O thou Love eternal,
shepherd of the wandering star and souls that wayward flee,
Homeward draws the spirit, to thy Spirit yearning,
Who wert, and art, and evermore shalt be."

III

Thou living God, from whom the whole family in heaven and on earth is named, we lift to thee—in vivid memory, in yearning recollection, in loving pride—the life of our friend and well-beloved and its earthly completion in death. We who are also strangers and sojourners on earth, sorrowing of heart and yet in quietness and confidence, in this room of sacred memories and fond hopes, turn to thee. It is as though many unseen bowed and prayed with us. This is a place whose walls and colors and music are a sacrament of remembrance, a place of beginnings and endings. It is a place of joys and sorrows shared, where sacrifices have been gladly made, burdens lightened, and resolutions strengthened; a place of aspiration and healing, of poignancy and peace, of truth wrestled with and faith recovered, of prayers answered and unanswered; a place where we have gotten again a grip on this strange business of living; a place of the coming in together of people to worship thee and of their going out to serve their generation in the name of Christ.

We bless thee, our Father in heaven, for all duty quietly and unostentatiously done,—with joy; for all leadership and charm; for affection freely given and modestly received; for love to the unlovely, and undiscouragable service to the ungrateful; for cheerful heart that doeth good like medicine.

Thanks be to thee, O God, for those who do great things with strength and small things graciously, who face each day without the backward glance of repining or despondency, who look upon themselves without pretense or evasion and turn from self-scrutiny to self-forgetfulness, who have discovered within themselves unsuspected resources of meditation and contentment, who keep the prison-walls of conventionality from closing in upon them; who, burdened by routine, beset by exacting obligation, yet manage to retain the consciousness of their place in thy vast design, so that their enterprises reflect thy magnanimity and patience; for those whose busy lives are not lives of busyness, who have discovered that not everyone who wants to help can be a helper, but that only those can bear another's burdens who are steadily and bravely bearing their own; for whom sentiment does not lapse into sentimentality; whose mature powers ripen into a harvest-tide of wisdom, upon which many draw for sustenance; whose assurance of the future is often hesitant and intermittent but who follow after, that they may lay hold of the prize for which also Christ has laid hold on us; who at the end have known an unclouded sunset, with its promise of a fair tomorrow.

We praise thee, O God, whose name is love and whose signature is a cross, for those who make it easier for us to believe in other people, and who make thee real to us; whose guiding hand has steadied many a young person trying to find her way,—his way to an abundant life, who have raised the sights of low ambition and brought hidden talents to light, who have known how to forgive follies and blunders; who omit none of the delicate attentions of friendship and whose radiance has brought us many a happy hour, smile and laugh; who have been strong to lean upon; who by their fidelity have banished many a calamity, by their merriment lightened many a burden, by their counsel averted many a disaster, by their sharing rendered many an anxiety bearable; who know how to be good companions.

We bless thee that lives built into each other by the painstaking handwork of mutual love and service, lives that touch not merely on the surface where change reigns but in the deep layers of soul and mind where thou art present,—such lives are built into thee and possess in thee an imperishable home. Those who abide in love abide in thee and in the house of thy love are many mansions. Part of our life's unalterable good they are. "They come transfigured back, secure from change in their high-hearted ways, Beautiful evermore, and with the rays of morn on their white shields of expectation."

Make thou our grief and our love, our loneliness and our pride a part of this Christmas season. May we, people that dwell in darkness, see again a great light. Upon us who dwell in the land of the shadow of death and who have walked beside so many who have entered into the valley of that shadow, let the light shine again, a light coming out of darkness, the light of life and immortality through the gospel, the burning and shining light of whom it was said, He could not be holden unto death, even Jesus Christ, who is the light of the world, the Christmas candle of the Lord of Hosts.

IV

Lord, our forebears in their pilgrimage walked by thy guidance and rested on thy compassion. Still to us, their children, be thou the pillar of cloud by day, the pillar of fire by night. Make a sanctuary within our hearts by thy presence there and humble us to kneel in the company of our inmost thoughts and grateful memories.

Thou who shinest in the illumined minds of all who seek truth, we bless thee for the goodly succession of teachers who have interpreted thy word to us and enriched us with its treasures; for painstaking scholars through whom law-givers, prophets and men of wisdom of many generations, being dead, yet speak freshly, to counsel and hearten the living; for the rich delight of well-furnished minds, for intellectual enthusiasm, for wit and good humor; for those who, conscious of the great heritage which is theirs, have participated in the struggles for faith and discernment on the part of men of older days, shared with us their achievements, failures, courages and despairs, their loyalties and disobedience, and made these men and women of God our contemporaries,—thus enlarging the cloud of witnesses which compass us about.

We bless thee for those for whom the rich resources of our Christian heritage have become second nature; for those who gladly enter into the memories and hopes of each institution they have served, feeling its momentum, shaping its future, making it a part of their own lives.

Let his memory abide in benediction among his former colleagues, his friends, and that larger company of students in many lands whose minds he enlarged, whose imaginations he quickened, whose faith he strengthened; and who hold him in reverent affection. Gather up now our silent prayers too deep for words, and keep us within the circle of Jesus Christ.

PSALM 23

Lord, thou has been his shepherd. He did not want. Thou didst make him to lie down in green pastures. Thou didst lead him beside the still waters. Thou didst restore his soul. Thou didst lead him in the paths of righteousness for thy name's sake. Yea, when he walked through the valley of the shadow of death, he feared no evil, for thou wast with him. Thy rod and thy staff, they comforted him. Thou didst prepare a table before him in the presence of his enemies; thou anointedst his head with oil. His cup ran over. Surely goodness and mercy have followed him all the days of his life and he now dwells in thy house, Lord, forever.

A MEMORIAL PRAYER

Lord, so recently have they bowed and prayed with us. They shared our days and nights. Living with us they brought to Pilgrim Place the rich experience of vigorous living. They did not leave it as they found it; they became a part of it; they molded it, criticized it, enriched it, kept it going. Living biographies they are of faith and hope and love, vivid, and energetic, patient and outgiving. The books they loved! The gardens they worked in! The services they rendered to us in this community and outside this place!

Each of us has a special grief, a private grief. Together we share a common sorrow, we acknowledge a common indebtedness, we are joined in a common gratefulness.

Lord, we who now live in Claremont, pray thy name.

In the name of the One who said a word we do not believe until we discover it is true, "Blessed are they that mourn," in the name of him who once lived in Nazareth.

A FAMILY COMMITAL SERVICE

Changed yet not broken is the inner circle of our family and the wider circle of dear friends gathered in the recurring pathos and promise of the passing years to carry out these last tender offices of faith and hope and love. It is as though many bowed and prayed with us.

We gather up in our minds those for whom we have mourned long since and now once again.

We lift up to thee, Lord, this experience of bereavement, as a common mold into which each of us pours our own private grief and our shared glory.

GRACES FOR A RETIREMENT COMMUNITY

Lord, with the psalmist-poet we exclaim, "How good and pleasant it is for us to dwell together" in the unity of fellowship, if not always of opinion.

How good and pleasant it is to dwell together in the fellowship of which these crowded tables in this familiar room are both experience and symbol.

Lord, we bless thee for those who bring thee with them as they come to this place; and leaving, take thee with them home.

For the nourishment of daily bread, we bless thee, Lord; for the nourishment of remembered moments which are also life and food for our diminished years; and for the in-between meals made up of all those "little unremembered acts of kindness and of love" that we receive.

Lord, they've done it again. Some of them, like some of us, bored, some not feeling too well, some cheerful, glad to have a job whose immediate results they can see, glad to have a helping kind of job. The food is ready in the kitchen, some of it already on the tray carts, all prepared under skillful management. The tables are set and flowered. And here we are, beneficiaries, not always sure we are any longer worth it, but leaving that in thy hands. Thank you, Lord.

Lord, we bless thee for all those who know that "earth's is not too poor to give us something to live for here that shall outlive us, something that gives our feeble light a high immunity from night, something that leaps life's narrow bars to claim its birthright with the hosts of heaven—a gladness fed with secret tears, a vexing forward-looking sense of some more noble permanence, a light across the sea which haunts our soul and will not let it be."

ACADEMIC

A COLLEGE CONVOCATION

Lord, we who have felt the impulse to create, we who have known the freedom of trusting in the truth, we who have been tied together with others in one bundle of affection and loyalty, we who have called injustice by its right name, we bless thee for those occasions,—mysterious and fascinating occasions,—when deep within us we have known thy name, for we have felt thy power: Creator, Spirit of Truth, Spirit of Love, Spirit of Good Will.

Enable us to discover—each one of us here—to discover the issue of our life, the cause for which we are here upon this earth, so that we may no longer, dull-spirited, bob about upon the surface of life, like driftwood upon the sea.

Save us in the days ahead from using our equipment of education and culture and friendship just for our own advancement and entertainment. Prepare us to place these gifts of ours at the service of our less endowed and less fortunate fellow men and women.

May our love of the earth and our love for people, like two hands washing each other, keep both clean and sweet.

Accustom us, as members of this College, to plan not only for its interests and effectiveness but also for the larger concerns of this community in which we live and for the happier destiny of mankind.

Thou, Alpha and Omega, who art the Beginning of all good beginnings and the End, the goal, of all good endings, Harbor and Horizon, in pride and thankfulness we bless thy holy name.

BEFORE AN ACADEMIC DINNER

O God, whose awesome name is Truth and whose Will is peace and freedom, on this recurrent festival of our University fellowship, we celebrate the long enterprise of human knowledge. We celebrate this community of scholars and teachers. Grant us the wisdom to comprehend and the courage to set forward the business of our common life.

A PREPARATORY SCHOOL COMMENCEMENT

Father almighty, we bless thee for this school, which has been the center of our interests, the guide of our activities, the molder of our growth in mind, in body and in spirit. How grateful we are for the friendships we have made here, for vistas of knowledge opening before us, for appreciation of things of beauty, for tastes cultivated and skills acquired, for teachers who somehow have won us to more decent living and clearer thinking by their teaching and example.

We see a fork ahead of us—two roads, a high road and a low road. May we have the nerve to choose, not that low road of self-conceit and self-indulgence, but instead choose the high road and get ready to place such abilities as we have enthusiastically at the disposal of people who desperately need our help. So in our turn, we may become persons who serve our generation in the spirit of Jesus Christ.

A COLLEGE CHAPEL INVOCATION

Once again, Lord, we will try to find the right words, each for himself, each for each other, and each with each other.

This strange passion for learning, for knowing more, knowing correctly, knowing straight,—whence comes it?

This ceaseless spinning of threads of connection between ourselves and others, ties,—fragile sometimes, transient sometimes, sometimes unbreakable,—whence come these fidelities?

This giving which is not a giving, for it is just being ourselves, this making available to others these talents of ours that they may yield delight or understanding or support,—whence comes this good will?

Thou art the giver of all these gifts.

We give thee especial thanks for this college, this tool for learning and knowing, this magnet for fidelity, this launching pad for the outgoing of good will.

A SEMINARY CONVOCATION

Eternal God, thee we praise from whom flow all the blessings of life and love, and for that special blessing which is our Seminary. For it we give thanks, and for our part in its enduring and on-going life. Help us to discover in it new dimensions of the Beloved Community of hope, of faith, of love. Teach us how, by the wise use of the passing hours, to bind its days each to the other, in the natural piety of time. Make us jealous for the great traditions of this institution that we may have confidence in its longer hopes. Keep clean and fresh its spiritual climate, that it may remain a place where students and teachers have confidence in each other and in the basic truth and effectiveness of the Christian faith. May we come to be trusted and believed in by one another, as we learn more about the ways in which human lives are controlled by the Christian gospel, incorporated into the Christian fellowship and steadied by the Christian heritage.

We pray for our teachers, who are at once the hope and the despair of their students. Arm them with the weapons of the spirit,—patience, humility, and devotion.

We pray for our students,—at once the despair and the hope of their teachers. May they welcome the disciplines of learning. Here may some deep truth which they have known about and repeated, come alive and seize them with its commanding significance.

We thank thee for those whose gifts across the years have made possible our work and worship here together on this campus; for those who live on through the inspiring teaching of a professor, made possible by their money; for those whose life is carried forward in the daily activity of students whose studying they have provided for; for those whose substance has been metamorphosed into books which concentrate the wisdom and learning of the past, an understanding of the present and an exploration of the paths of the spirit ahead. God bless us all.

SEMINARY CHAPEL SERVICES

I

Heavenly Father, we present ourselves before thee, a company of students and teachers, each with individual decisions confronting us, with separate hopes, with personal anxieties, with our cynicisms and doubts, with the trusts others have in us, the obligations we have undertaken, the causes that burn into our attention, and all of us alike standing in the need of knowing each other, for we belong together by common interests shared, by common goals set before us, by common incentives for service, by common hungers and thirsts for the living water. We are a cluster of islands, each with our own geology and landscape, yet each a part of the solid continent below.

So, by our common praise and our common prayer, may we place our lives again in thy hands and rediscover our belonging together in the Christian fellowship of this Seminary.

II

Draw near to us, Lord, teach us and guide us:
by the inscrutable wonders of thy universe,
by the promptings of our grateful hearts,
by the exacting responsibilities conscience forces us to assume,
by strong ties of happy friendships,
by shame at opportunities misused,
by bitter lessons of experience,
by second chances given us,
by all fair memories and fond hopes,
by every impulse to do our best for the sake of others,
by the good examples of thy servants,
by the abiding memory of Jesus in the world,
Draw near to each of us and tighten the bonds of fellowship among us who are teachers and students here together.

III

Our praying, Lord, is a stripping away of the labels by which we are classified. Before thee we are not professors and students, younger people and older people, activists and reflectives.

Our praying together is a striving to acknowledge our common level of creaturesness, our common brotherhood, our common birthright as thy children.

Our praying for these next few moments will be together keeping silence before thee. . . . . .

IV

Thou, who givest to everyone his calling as a means of serving thee, seeing we are compassed about with so great a cloud of witnesses, enable us to strip off the impediments in our wills, the entanglements of sin, the handicaps of attractive diversions. Enable us to run the appointed course of our studies and teaching and administration with determination, fixing our eyes on Jesus, leader and exemplar of our faith,—ourselves not free from conflicts and defeats but enduring the hardships of our calling as good soliders of Jesus Christ. So may we discover and rediscover the joy that is reserved for those who have dedicated themselves to thy service,—the joy of making plain to others the way that has been hard to find, the contentment of self-forgetfulness, the glad desire to live as those who come not to be ministered unto but to minister, giving our lives as a ransom for many.

V

Lord, thou hast set before us the shining goals of truth and knowledge, of wisdom, of fellowship, of adoration. Thou hast made *us* heirs of a great heritage.

We lift up to thee the long memories of this Seminary, of its founders and their successors across the decades, memories of men and women who have made its life a part of their own lives and whose devotion and strength have become living stones in this temple of the spirit of truth.

We bless thee for our belonging together here,—in common indebtnesses shared, in a love which demands of us high levels of performance, in incentives of gratitude, in recollections of vivid hours, in responses to the issues and appeals of thy kingdom to come on earth as it has come in heaven.

FOR THE MEMBERS OF A GRADUATING CLASS

God and Father of all men, source of truth and goodness, whose best gifts are minds to use and ambition to use them, a cause to give ourselves to, partners to work with, a Lord to serve; Alpha and Omega, the Beginning and the Ending. We lift up to thee the hopes consummated here, the sacrifices, the love and devotion which enfold these men and women. Receive their dedication here renewed. Give them faith enough to live by. Set them continuously in the great succession of thy ministers, that they may enter into the communion of the Christian generations. Bind them to their tasks with cords of love and discernment. Uphold them in patience and indefatigable hopefulness. May they enter into the happiness of spiritual authority and use it to do justly and to love mercy. Arm them for their high vocation with diligent and open minds, with the sword of the spirit that disarms controversy by character. Save them from bigotry and dogmatism. Accustom their daily thoughts to dwell on thy purposes and laws. As now they rise up with wings like eagles, so may they run the course of their careers and not be weary, and, when the days of retirement come, may they walk and not faint. Be still for them the God of Good Hope. Be for them the Captain of Victory.

AT AN ANNUAL MEETING

Lord, how astonishing, at times, are our routines when we take time to pray about them.

Here we are, again, meeting together, not to eat, not to raise money, not to be entertained, but to review the actions of our common life together, to learn about the work our elected leaders have carried on in our behalf. We shall be likely to wonder why this or that was done, why this or that was not done. We expect at times to be bored. We expect also the exhilaration we feel when a fresh idea is voiced.

Most of all and underlying all, we shall be praising thee in whom all things are held together, praising thee at the front of our minds, praising thee at the back of our minds, praising thee for decisions made, for initiatives taken, for volunteerings, for responsibilities accepted,—all of which are [this organization's] ways of spelling love and engaging in acts of love. Lord, God of Glory! God of Love!

INVOCATION AT A BUSINESS CONFERENCE

Amidst our confusions and competitions, beset by detail and routine, burdened by the anxieties and perplexities of the days' work, we name thy name, God, not as a curse, not as an idle word, not in vain but seeking a blessing, God, that we may recover a sense of our places in thy vast design, a sense of the contribution our business makes to human welfare.

Commentary

PUBLIC PRAYER AS A FORM OF LITERARY ART

Speaking to their Condition. Dr. George A. Gordon, when he was minister of the New Old South Church in Boston, tells of a parishioner greeting him after the morning service: "Dr. Gordon, I like your sermons to be pointed, but is it fair to point at me?"

Like Dr. Gordon's sermons these prayers are pointed. They point, however, not in condemnation but in recognition. They point to and point up a wide spectrum of human experiences. People who listen are likely to recognize that some part of a prayer points to their particular condition or to someone they know. They are glad, not indignant.

These prayers are not sermons in disguise. They are not statements of belief. They are infrequently informative. They are an attempt rather on the part of the leader to bring into focus, in cameo-like expression, feelings and attitudes which are present in the minds and hearts of the congregation. Thus the leader is praying with the people, individually and as a community of fellow-prayers, and they hopefully are praying with him.

Initials in the Margins. It was the practice of a young minister in the early part of the 19th century, whenever in his sermon he described some attitude or mood, to put in the margin of his manuscript the initials of the person who exemplified or reminded him of such a characteristic. In the margins of these prayers are many invisible sets of initials.

My "bank". Dr. Coffin once urged leaders of worship to keep a loose-leafed notebook in which to enter phrases from the Bible and other books that suggest material for public prayers. My "bank book" contains deposits from novels, poetry, plays and biographies, which I have drawn upon while composing many of these prayers.

Vocabulary. Dr. Charles W. Gilkey, when Dean of the Chapel of the University of Chicago, tells of a sermon delivered by a famous Scots minister which was a rich and colorful tapestry woven of Biblical quotations and allusions in which the scriptural scenes and characters subtly emerged into a unified and cumulative processing as the well-planned sermon unrolled. In the middle of the sermon a graduate student in physics got up and went out, sat down on the steps outside and began to read the *Chicago Tribune.* When a passing student asked him why he had left the Chapel, he replied, 'I will not stay and listen to a man who cannot talk about religion in a language which his contemporaries can understand?" (*Protestant Thought in the 20th Century*, p. 217 ed. by Arnold S. Nash)

For the members of many other American congregations and academic assemblies the Bible has ceased to be primary reading matter. It appears to me that Biblical language can no longer be counted on to touch the cords of memory and reenforce spiritual security as it used to when the Biblical vocabulary was almost a second language. The increasing familiarity with new translations has also meant that the words and rhythms of the King James translation and even of the Revised Version are losing their currency. These observations probably explain the predominance of non-Biblical imagery and language and the relative paucity of Biblical words and phrases in these prayers.

Subjunctives. The use of "might" and "would" instead of "may" and "will" has become the distinctive style of many of the prayers in today's services of worship. How this has come about I do not know; nor when. The subjunctive mood is a verbal form indicating doubt, uncertainty, possibility. Justification for its use in prayers is infrequent.

Pronouns. I make no apology for continuing a life-long habit of using the pronouns "thou," "thee," "thy" when addressing God. An interesting linguistic reversal is rapidly taking place in contemporary services of worship. Formerly "thou" etc. were a form of familiarity as opposed to the more formal "you." Now "you" is becoming the familiar form. Much as I deplore having to admit it, I remain a traditionalist at this point. This surprises me, as I have long thought of myself rather as an iconoclast.

Gender. Many of these prayers were composed before the time when sensitive leaders in the churches, under the influence of the feminist movement, began to use the feminine gender when referring to or addressing God, as well as to find substitutes for the generic use of the word "man" in such terms as mankind. I find myself uncomfortable in these changes of gender. And this is spite of the fact that early in my ministry I became acquainted with the powerful prayers of a notable Boston preacher, Theodore Parker, first published cir. 1860. He address God sometimes as Father, sometimes as Mother, sometimes as both.

Questions in Prayers. If a precedent is needed for this style of discourse, see Saint Augustine's *Confessions,* and the Book of Psalms.

Quotation Marks. Obviously they cannot be indicated in spoken prayers. Should they appear in printed prayers? Certainly not, in the case of quotations from the Bible. Where I am aware of using other sources I have either included quotation marks or indented the quoted passage.

Punctuation. Printed language is at a disadvantage in comparison with a musical score. Both have available notations and signs. Print uses punctuation. Periods, commas, indentations, etc. indicate ways in which the succession of words is to be understood. A musical score also has notations. Staves, clefs, rests, size and design of notes, etc. indicate how the composer intends the music to be played or sung. A musical score has additional notations such as tempi (relative speed), dynamics (degree of loudness), and phrasings (groupings of sound). I have often wished that such notations as these had their equivalents in print, to serve as guidance for anyone who speaks the words out loud. Just as a sermon is not a sermon until it is preached so a public prayer is not a prayer until it is spoken.

Silences. In the Roman Mass it is customary for the worshippers, while the priest in the chancel is engaged in the litany, to say their beads. Protestant tradition assumes that worshippers will make their own the words of the leader of worship. Neither practice provides for the periods of silence which are a major feature of worship as carried on by the Society of Friends. A few of these prayers pay minimal recognition to the Quaker insight.

Conclusions. I have not followed the tradition of concluding these prayers with one of the common phrases, such as "In Jesus' name," "In the spirit of Christ," "For Christ's sake," "through Jesus Christ."

1. "In the name of Jesus" smacks of magic. Fairy tales tell of a magic formula that would open a cave or unlock a door, "Open Sesame." My mind is inhospitable to magic.

2. "In the spirit of Jesus." The appropriate place for this is at the beginning of a prayer, as a reminder to the pray-er of the quality of the prayer he is about to say. If a prayer has not been permeated with the spirit of Jesus, the invocation of his name at the end will not make it so.

3. "For Jesus' sake," "Through Jesus Christ," I find theologically obscure.

So I have assumed that you who have read thus far have added your own conclusions. I am comforted in my omissions by the observation that in the retirement community where I live alongside some three hundred men and women whose lives have been devoted to "professional Christian service," with increasing frequency these traditional conclusions are omitted from public prayers, at table and at Vespers.

Amen. When asked why in the morning service he had gone on and on and on in the "long" prayer, the minister confessed, "Well, I just couldn't remember the word Amen." Amen has become a sound which signifies that the prayer has ended, except in congregations which are given occasional instruction in the meaning of the successive parts of the liturgy. Such people are informed that the word has several meanings in the Bible. Amen is predominantly an exclamation signifying support, assent, approval. As such it is an appropriate interjection on the part of the congregation. When at a revival meeting people shout Amen, they are telling the preacher that he has made a strong point with which they heartily agree. In so far as the word

Amen continues to carry this meaning, its use by the person who has delivered the prayer seems inappropriate, if not ridiculous. He is saying, in effect, "I heartily agree with and support what I have just said." The use of an Amen also relieves the composer of a prayer of the necessity of ending it with a climax. There appears to be small justification, except tradition, for continuing to use it.

Generalities. My emphasis on concreteness in public prayers by no means deprecates the value, indeed the unavoidability, of generalities in liturgical worship where the same prayers are repeated week after week, often in unison. Such magnificent prayers as the General Confession ("Almighty and most merciful Father. . .") and the General Thanksgiving ("Almighty God, Father of all mercies. . .") are moulds into which individual worshippers may pour their specific needs and concerns. Such recurrent prayers, also, like the repetition of a creed, serve other purposes. They are a kind of flag which indicates where the worshippers' loyalty lies. They revive the sense of belonging, of being reincorporated into the church with all the supportive memories and experiences pertaining thereto.

Other Books of Prayers. Their number is legion. One only of them do I find difficulty in not mentioning, for it has an Introduction which I should like to have borrowed for my own. In it Harry Emerson Fosdick writes: "In non-liturgical churches the minister does not kneel in the chancel, facing the altar, as though addressing himself to the Most High. He stands in the pulpit, facing the congregation. That obvious fact defines his function in public prayer. He is trying so to phrase the souls's adoration, thanksgiving, penitence, petitions, and intercessions, that the people may be caught up into his prayer and may themselves pray with him." He goes on to characterize some of the so-called pastoral prayers: "Some deal with generalities, and do not come to grips with specific needs. They ask foregiveness for sins, but do not say what sins. They express gratitude for blessings but do not name the blessings. . . . . . Some prayers are Sunday after Sunday a repetitious rehearsal of the same petitions in much the same words. . . . No wonder that prayer time is often put to somnolent use." He concludes these comments on "well-worn cliches" and "verbal formality": they lack "the freshness, radiance and challenge of genuine prayer." (*A Book of Public Prayers,* Harpers, 1959, pp. 7f.)